DATE DUE

GAYLORD   PRINTED IN U.S.A.

CRICKETS IN THE DARK

Doreen Gonzales

PowerKiDS
press.

New York

Published in 2010 by The Rosen Publishing Group, Inc.
29 East 21st Street, New York, NY 10010

First Edition

Editor: Amelie von Zumbusch
Book Design: Julio Gil
Photo Researcher: Jessica Gerweck

Photo Credits: Cover Norbert Wu/Getty Images; pp. 5, 9, 17 Shutterstock.com; p. 6 © Anthony Bannister; Gallo Images/Corbis; p. 10 Joel Sartore/Getty Images; p. 13 Altrendo Nature/Getty Images; p. 14 © Juniors Bildarchiv/age fotostock; p. 18 © Chris Mattison; Frank Lane Picture Agency/Corbis; p. 21 Sean Justice/Getty Images.

Library of Congress Cataloging-in-Publication Data

Gonzales, Doreen.
  Crickets in the dark / Doreen Gonzales. — 1st ed.
    p. cm. — (Creatures of the night)
  Includes index.
  ISBN 978-1-4042-8098-4 (library binding) — ISBN 978-1-4358-3253-4 (pbk.) — ISBN 978-1-4358-3254-1 (6-pack)
  1. Crickets—Juvenile literature. I. Title.
  QL508.G8G66 2010
  595.7'26—dc22
                                              2009000483

Manufactured in the United States of America

CONTENTS

CRICKETS ARE EVERYWHERE!

What is that chirping sound in the grass on summer nights? It must be crickets! Most crickets are **nocturnal**. These **insects** spend their days sleeping in the grass and under logs. At night, they come out to eat and sing. A few kinds of crickets are **crepuscular**. They begin their songs as the Sun sets.

There are thousands of kinds of crickets. The largest are about 2 inches (5 cm) long. The littlest crickets are smaller than many ants. Crickets live almost everywhere in the world. These singing insects can be found in forests, fields, trees, backyards, gardens, buildings, and even under ground.

As all insects do, crickets have six legs and compound eyes. Compound eyes are made up of many little parts that take in light. These eyes are good at sensing movement.

LEGS WITH EARS

Most crickets are black or brown. These dark colors hide crickets from nighttime **predators**. Some crickets are gray or light green. This makes them hard to see against the rocks or leaves where they hide during the day.

Crickets have six legs. The insects' four front legs are shorter than the two in back. A cricket's ears are on its two front legs!

Crickets have two long **antennae** coming from their heads. These antennae are often longer than a cricket's body is! Crickets use antennae to feel what is around them. This is very helpful in the dark.

Their very long antennae are one way to tell crickets apart from other jumping insects, such as grasshoppers.

A HARD SHELL

A cricket's body is covered with a hard shell, called an **exoskeleton**. Its exoskeleton holds a cricket's soft body parts and keeps them from getting hurt. Cricket exoskeletons have three parts. These are a head, a **thorax**, and a long **abdomen**.

Crickets outgrow their exoskeletons many times as they grow. Each time a cricket gets too big for its shell, the exoskeleton breaks open. The cricket crawls out of its shell and a new, larger exoskeleton grows around the cricket. This is called molting. A cricket grows a little bigger each time it molts. After its last molt, the cricket is an adult.

You can see the three parts of this cricket's body here. The thorax, or middle part, is where the animal's wings and legs join its body.

THE WIDE WORLD OF CRICKETS

There are hundreds of kinds of crickets. Field crickets are common. They live in fields, yards, and buildings. These black or brown crickets are about 1.3 inches (33 mm) long. House crickets can also be found in many places. They like to live in buildings where they can stay warm.

Mole crickets live in underground tunnels that they dig. They come out at night to gather leaves and grasses. Tree crickets live in trees and bushes. People can figure out the exact **temperature** by counting the chirps of the snowy tree cricket. As other crickets do, it chirps more quickly in warm weather.

This tree cricket was found in Nebraska. Tree crickets are quite small. They generally grow to be only .5 inch (13 mm) long.

Jumping to Safety

Most kinds of crickets have two pairs of wings. These crickets' wings lie flat on their backs. Even though most kinds of crickets have wings, many crickets cannot fly. Crickets generally jump or crawl to get where they want to go.

Crickets use their strong back legs to jump away from danger. Nocturnal predators often lose sight of crickets after they jump into the darkness. Many crickets can jump 20 times their own length! Can you imagine jumping over 20 people your own size while they were lying head to toe? Crickets also use their powerful back legs to kick at animals that are trying to catch them.

As all insects do, crickets have legs with several segments, or parts. These segments let a cricket bend its powerful back legs when it gets ready to jump.

A CRICKET SONG

Only male crickets chirp. Some crickets chirp only at night. Others sing in the daytime, too. Many crickets chirp a lot in the late summer and early fall. Crickets chirp with their wings. Male crickets have a row of teeth like those on a comb along the bottom of one wing. A **scraper** lines the bottom of the other wing. To chirp, a cricket rubs the scraper on one wing along the teeth on the other.

Male crickets chirp each night to call females to them. Sometimes they chirp to tell other males to get away. Each kind of cricket has its own song.

People who study crickets have learned that male field crickets of the kind seen here chirp more often when they have found lots of food to eat.

All crickets begin life as an egg. Some types of crickets lay their eggs in soil. Other kinds lay eggs in tree bark or on plant leaves or stems. Female crickets of many kinds lay their eggs just before the coldest part of the year. The eggs stay there until the weather warms and baby crickets **hatch** from them.

Baby crickets are called nymphs. Nymphs look a lot like adult crickets. Nymphs molt many times before they are fully grown. Crickets often molt between 8 and 10 times. Crickets do not have very long lives. Some crickets live only for a few weeks. Other kinds of crickets die when the weather turns cold.

You can tell cricket nymphs, such as this one, from adults because the nymphs have either no wings or wings that are just starting to grow.

Eating Crickets

Crickets are **omnivorous**. This means that they eat both plants and animals. Crickets eat grass, leaves, seeds, and smaller insects. Crickets have also been known to eat dead animals and even other crickets. Crickets that live indoors will feed on cloth, leather, and paper.

Their nocturnal ways keep crickets safe from some daytime predators. However, several nighttime predators, such as birds, spiders, skunks, raccoons, and foxes, eat crickets.

People eat crickets, too. There are some people who like **chocolate**-covered crickets. In several places, crickets are an important kind of meat. People in these places often eat crickets fried.

Some of the predators that crickets have to watch out for are the praying mantids. These large insects are skillful hunters.

PEOPLE AND CRICKETS

In many places, crickets are thought to bring good luck. Some people keep male crickets because they like to hear the crickets' chirping. They put the crickets in cages so they can listen to their nighttime songs.

People also use crickets as pet food. They feed them to their frogs, turtles, and lizards. In some parts of the world, people enjoy watching crickets fight. They cage male crickets and feed them lots of healthy food. When they want to watch a fight, the people put two crickets together and make them angry. The crickets fight, sometimes even killing each other.

These girls are looking at their pet cricket. People in Japan and China have raised pet crickets for thousands of years.

NIGHTS FULL OF SONG

At times, crickets can be pests. These insects sometimes find their way into homes and bother people. Outside, large numbers of crickets can destroy crops and other plants.

However, crickets are an important part of nature. Many birds and animals need crickets for food. Crickets also help keep Earth's soil healthy. The insects' bodies break up the plants they eat and produce droppings, which go into the soil and make it rich. This makes plants grow better.

Crickets are not only useful, but they also make our lives more agreeable. Their beautiful chirping fills summer nights with song!

GLOSSARY

ABDOMEN (AB-duh-mun) The large, back part of an insect's body.

ANTENNAE (an-TEH-nee) Thin, rodlike feelers located on the heads of certain animals.

CHOCOLATE (CHAH-kuh-let) Candy made from cooked cacao beans.

CREPUSCULAR (krih-PUS-kyuh-lur) Active just before sunrise and just after sunset.

EXOSKELETON (ek-soh-SKEH-leh-tun) The hard covering on the outside of an animal's body that holds and guards the soft insides.

HATCH (HACH) To come out of an egg.

INSECTS (IN-sekts) Small animals that often have six legs and wings.

NOCTURNAL (nok-TUR-nul) Active during the night.

OMNIVOROUS (om-NIV-rus) Eating both plants and animals.

PREDATORS (PREH-duh-terz) Animals that kill other animals for food.

SCRAPER (SKRAYP-er) Something that rubs against or tears something else.

TEMPERATURE (TEM-pur-cher) How hot or cold something is.

THORAX (THOR-aks) The middle part of the body of an insect. The wings and legs come from the thorax.

INDEX

A
antennae, 7

B
backyards, 4
birds, 22

E
ears, 7
egg(s), 16
exoskeleton, 8

F
females, 15
fields, 11

G
gardens, 4
grass(es), 4, 11, 19

L
leaves, 7, 16, 19
legs, 7, 12
luck, 20

N
nymphs, 16

R
raccoons, 19
rocks, 7

S
seeds, 19
skunks, 19
soil, 22
song(s), 15, 20, 22
spiders, 19

T
teeth, 15
thorax, 8
turtles, 20

W
weather, 11, 16
wing(s), 12, 15

WEB SITES

Due to the changing nature of Internet links, PowerKids Press has developed an online list of Web sites related to the subject of this book. This site is updated regularly. Please use this link to access the list: www.powerkidslinks.com/cnight/cricket/